**Editor**

Mary S. Jones

**Managing Editor**

Karen J. Goldfluss, M.S. Ed.

**Illustrator**

Blanca Apodaca

**Cover Artist**

Barb Lorseyedi

**Art Production Manager**

Kevin Barnes

**Art Coordinator**

Renée Christine Yates

**Imaging**

James Edward Grace

Ricardo A. Martinez

**Publisher**

Mary D. Smith, M.S. Ed.

# Math Picture Puzzles

## GRADE 1

Teacher Created Resources

**Author**

*Mary Rosenberg*

*Teacher Created Resources, Inc.*

6421 Industry Way

Westminster, CA 92683

www.teachercreated.com

**ISBN: 978-1-4206-3906-3**

*©2006 Teacher Created Resources, Inc.*

Reprinted, 2014

Made in U.S.A.

# Table of Contents

Introduction. . . . . . . . . . . . . . . . . . . . . . . . . . . . . . . . . . . . . . . . . . . . . . . . . . . . . . . . . . . . . . 3

Puzzle 1:  Pizza, Pizza . . . . . . . . . . . . . . . . . . . . . . . . . . . . . . . . . . . . . . . . . . . . . . . . . . 4

Puzzle 2:  Howdy! . . . . . . . . . . . . . . . . . . . . . . . . . . . . . . . . . . . . . . . . . . . . . . . . . . . . . . 5

Puzzle 3:  Turtle Time. . . . . . . . . . . . . . . . . . . . . . . . . . . . . . . . . . . . . . . . . . . . . . . . . . . 6

Puzzle 4:  Slithering By . . . . . . . . . . . . . . . . . . . . . . . . . . . . . . . . . . . . . . . . . . . . . . . . . . 7

Puzzle 5:  Colorful Gumballs . . . . . . . . . . . . . . . . . . . . . . . . . . . . . . . . . . . . . . . . . . . . . 8

Puzzle 6:  Grandma's Quilt. . . . . . . . . . . . . . . . . . . . . . . . . . . . . . . . . . . . . . . . . . . . . . . 9

Puzzle 7:  Top of the Morning to You! . . . . . . . . . . . . . . . . . . . . . . . . . . . . . . . . . . . . . 10

Puzzle 8:  A Lazy Summer Day . . . . . . . . . . . . . . . . . . . . . . . . . . . . . . . . . . . . . . . . . . 11

Puzzle 9:  Give Me a 1, 2, 3! . . . . . . . . . . . . . . . . . . . . . . . . . . . . . . . . . . . . . . . . . . . . 12

Puzzle 10:  Numbers of the Sea . . . . . . . . . . . . . . . . . . . . . . . . . . . . . . . . . . . . . . . . . . 13

Puzzle 11:  Come Fly Away with Me . . . . . . . . . . . . . . . . . . . . . . . . . . . . . . . . . . . . . . 14

Puzzle 12:  Farmer's Market. . . . . . . . . . . . . . . . . . . . . . . . . . . . . . . . . . . . . . . . . . . . . 15

Puzzle 13:  Double Scoops . . . . . . . . . . . . . . . . . . . . . . . . . . . . . . . . . . . . . . . . . . . . . 16

Puzzle 14:  Robbie Robot . . . . . . . . . . . . . . . . . . . . . . . . . . . . . . . . . . . . . . . . . . . . . . . 17

Puzzle 15:  Busy as a Bee. . . . . . . . . . . . . . . . . . . . . . . . . . . . . . . . . . . . . . . . . . . . . . . 18

Puzzle 16:  Home Sweet Home . . . . . . . . . . . . . . . . . . . . . . . . . . . . . . . . . . . . . . . . . . 19

Puzzle 17:  Fluttering By . . . . . . . . . . . . . . . . . . . . . . . . . . . . . . . . . . . . . . . . . . . . . . . . 20

Puzzle 18:  Buzzing Through the Numbers . . . . . . . . . . . . . . . . . . . . . . . . . . . . . . . . . 21

Puzzle 19:  Over the Rainbow . . . . . . . . . . . . . . . . . . . . . . . . . . . . . . . . . . . . . . . . . . . 22

Puzzle 20:  Blooming Buds . . . . . . . . . . . . . . . . . . . . . . . . . . . . . . . . . . . . . . . . . . . . . 23

Puzzle 21:  Camping Out . . . . . . . . . . . . . . . . . . . . . . . . . . . . . . . . . . . . . . . . . . . . . . . 24

Puzzle 22:  Stripes for Dad. . . . . . . . . . . . . . . . . . . . . . . . . . . . . . . . . . . . . . . . . . . . . . 25

Puzzle 23:  Toucan Tom . . . . . . . . . . . . . . . . . . . . . . . . . . . . . . . . . . . . . . . . . . . . . . . . 26

Puzzle 24:  Box Full of Colors . . . . . . . . . . . . . . . . . . . . . . . . . . . . . . . . . . . . . . . . . . . 27

Puzzle 25:  Take Note! . . . . . . . . . . . . . . . . . . . . . . . . . . . . . . . . . . . . . . . . . . . . . . . . . 28

Puzzle 26:  Rat-A-Tat-Tat. . . . . . . . . . . . . . . . . . . . . . . . . . . . . . . . . . . . . . . . . . . . . . . 29

Puzzle 27:  Pennies, Nickels, and Dimes . . . . . . . . . . . . . . . . . . . . . . . . . . . . . . . . . . 30

Puzzle 28:  Money on the Flag . . . . . . . . . . . . . . . . . . . . . . . . . . . . . . . . . . . . . . . . . . . 31

Puzzle 29:  Follow the Arrow . . . . . . . . . . . . . . . . . . . . . . . . . . . . . . . . . . . . . . . . . . . . 32

Puzzle 30:  Blast Off! . . . . . . . . . . . . . . . . . . . . . . . . . . . . . . . . . . . . . . . . . . . . . . . . . . 33

Puzzle 31:  At the Barn. . . . . . . . . . . . . . . . . . . . . . . . . . . . . . . . . . . . . . . . . . . . . . . . . 34

Puzzle 32:  On the Road. . . . . . . . . . . . . . . . . . . . . . . . . . . . . . . . . . . . . . . . . . . . . . . . . 35

Puzzle 33:  Odd and Even . . . . . . . . . . . . . . . . . . . . . . . . . . . . . . . . . . . . . . . . . . . . . . . 36

Puzzle 34:  The Opposite Twins. . . . . . . . . . . . . . . . . . . . . . . . . . . . . . . . . . . . . . . . . . 37

Puzzle 35:  By the 2's . . . . . . . . . . . . . . . . . . . . . . . . . . . . . . . . . . . . . . . . . . . . . . . . . . 38

Puzzle 36:  It's Heavy! . . . . . . . . . . . . . . . . . . . . . . . . . . . . . . . . . . . . . . . . . . . . . . . . . 39

Puzzle 37:  Give a Cheer! . . . . . . . . . . . . . . . . . . . . . . . . . . . . . . . . . . . . . . . . . . . . . . . 40

Puzzle 38:  On the Island . . . . . . . . . . . . . . . . . . . . . . . . . . . . . . . . . . . . . . . . . . . . . . . 41

Answer Key . . . . . . . . . . . . . . . . . . . . . . . . . . . . . . . . . . . . . . . . . . . . . . . . . . . . . . . . 42–48

# Introduction

The old adage "practice makes perfect" can really hold true for your child and his or her education. The more practice and exposure your child has with concepts being taught in school, the more success he or she is likely to find. For many parents, knowing how to help your children can be frustrating because the resources may not be readily available. As a parent it is also difficult to know where to focus your efforts so that the extra practice your child receives at home supports what he or she is learning in school.

This book has been designed to help both parents and teachers reinforce basic math skills. *Practice Makes Perfect* reviews basic math skills for children in grade 1. This book contains math picture puzzles that allow children to learn, review, and reinforce basic math concepts. While it would be impossible to include all concepts taught in grade 1 in this book, the following main objectives are reinforced through practice exercises:

- addition
- counting
- money
- number words

- odd & even numbers
- patterns
- skip counting
- subtraction

There are 38 picture puzzles organized sequentially, so children can build their knowledge from more basic skills to higher-level math skills. Math picture puzzles are designed for students to review math concepts and have fun practicing them.

## How to Make the Most of This Book

Here are some useful ideas for optimizing the practice pages in this book:

- Set aside a specific place in your home to work on the practice pages. Keep it neat and tidy with materials on hand.

- Set up a certain time of day to work on the puzzles. This will establish consistency. An alternative is to look for times in your day or week that are less hectic and conducive to practicing skills.

- Keep all practice sessions with your child positive and constructive. If the mood becomes tense, or you and your child are frustrated, set the book aside and look for another time to practice with your child.

- Help with instructions if necessary. If your child is having difficulty understanding what to do or how to get started, work through the first problem with him or her.

- Review the work your child has done. This serves as reinforcement and provides further practice.

- Pay attention to the areas in which your child has the most difficulty. Provide extra guidance and exercises in those areas. Allowing children to use drawings and manipulatives, such as coins, tiles, or flash cards, can help them grasp difficult concepts more easily.

- Look for ways to make real-life applications to the skills being reinforced.

# Puzzle 1

## Pizza, Pizza

Count the dots.  Color the puzzle.

| 1 = red | 2 = brown | 3 = yellow | 4 = blue |

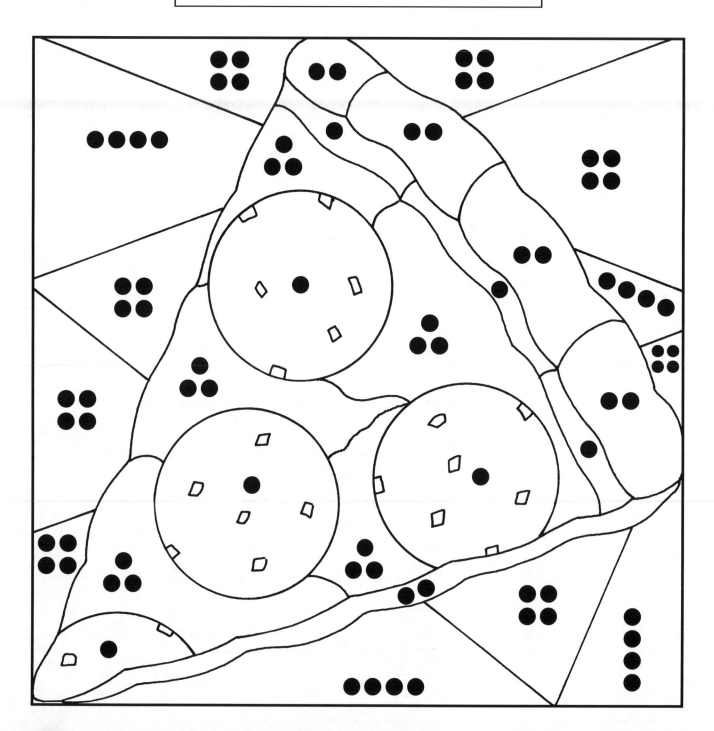

# Puzzle 4

## Slithering By

Name each number.  Color the puzzle.

| |
|---|
| zero = green    one = yellow    two = blue |

# Puzzle 5

## Colorful Gumballs

Name each number. Color the puzzle.

| | | | |
|---|---|---|---|
| three = red | four = orange | five = yellow | six = green |

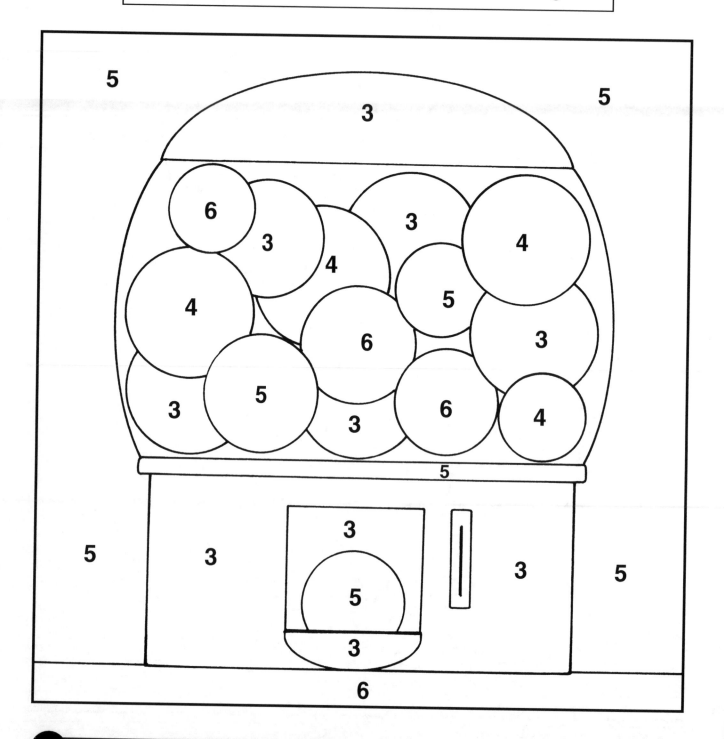

# Puzzle 6

## Grandma's Quilt

Name each number.  Color the puzzle.

> **seven = purple   eight = blue   nine = green   ten = red**

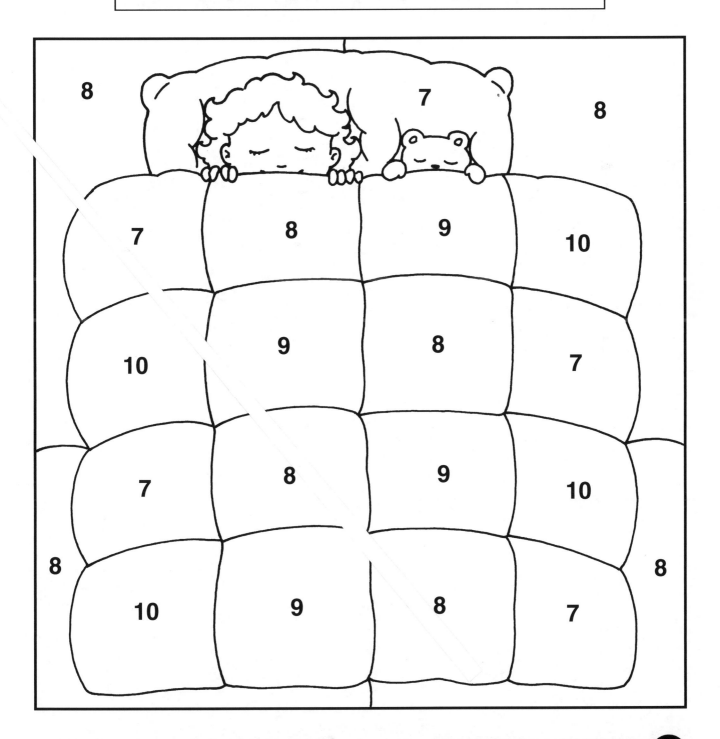

# Puzzle 7

## Top of the Morning to You!

Name each number.  Color the puzzle.

| | |
|---|---|
| **eleven = green   twelve = black   thirteen = red** | |
| **fourteen = orange   fifteen = yellow   sixteen = blue** | |

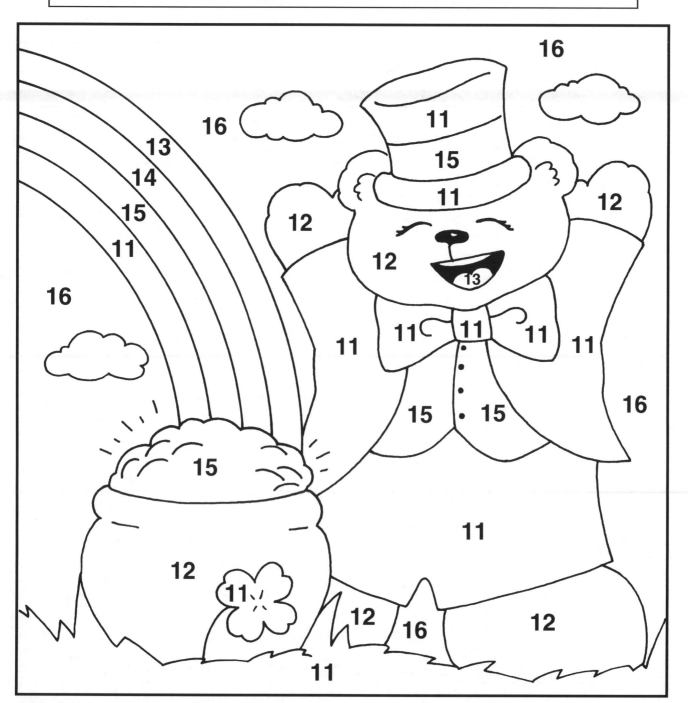

# Puzzle 8

## A Lazy Summer Day

Name each number.  Color the puzzle.

> **sixteen = yellow**   **seventeen = brown**   **eighteen = green**
> **nineteen = blue**   **twenty = purple**

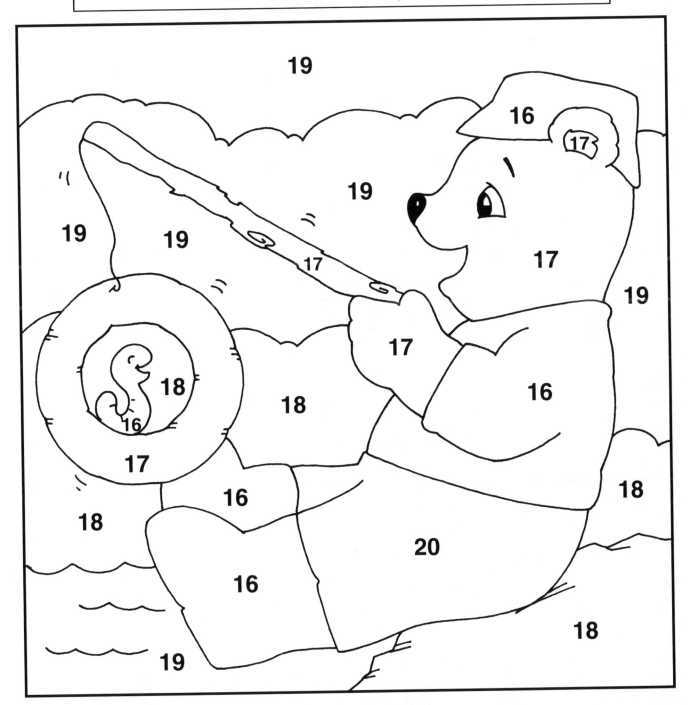

# Puzzle 9

## Give Me a 1, 2, 3!

Read each number word.  Color the puzzle.

| 0 = purple   1 = red   2 = blue   3 = gray |
| --- |

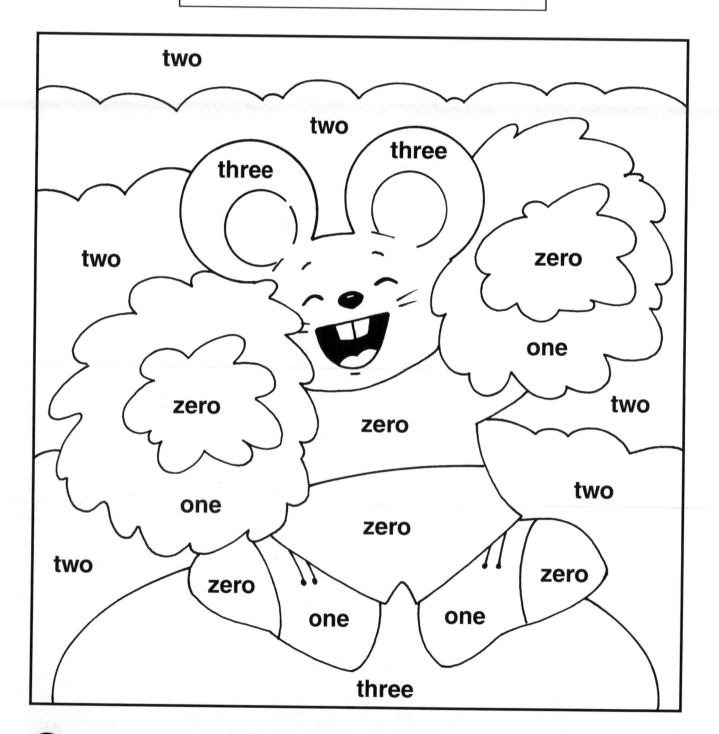

# Puzzle 10

## Numbers of the Sea

Read each number word.  Color the puzzle.

| 4 = blue   5 = green   6 = purple |
| --- |

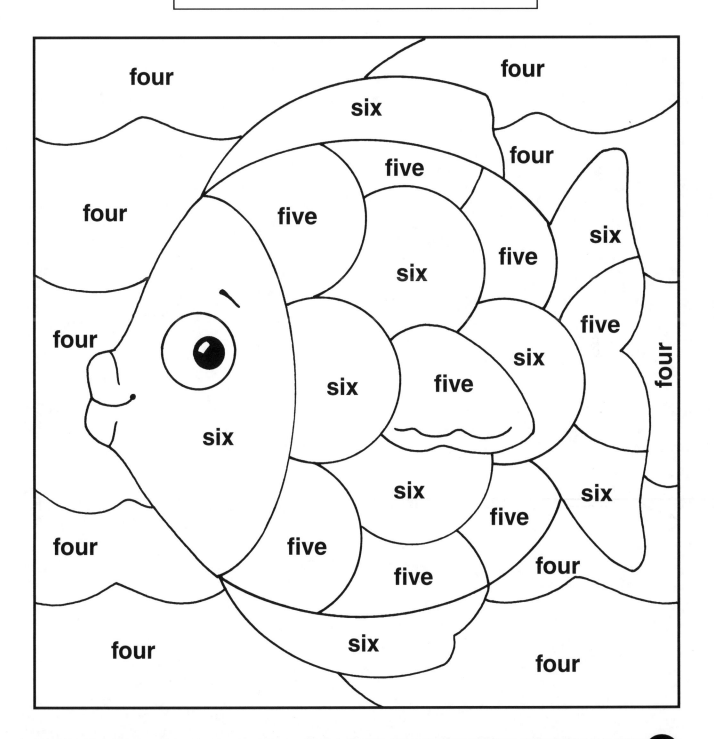

# Puzzle 11

## Come Fly Away with Me

Read each number word.  Color the puzzle.

```
7 = red    8 = brown    9 = blue    10 = green
```

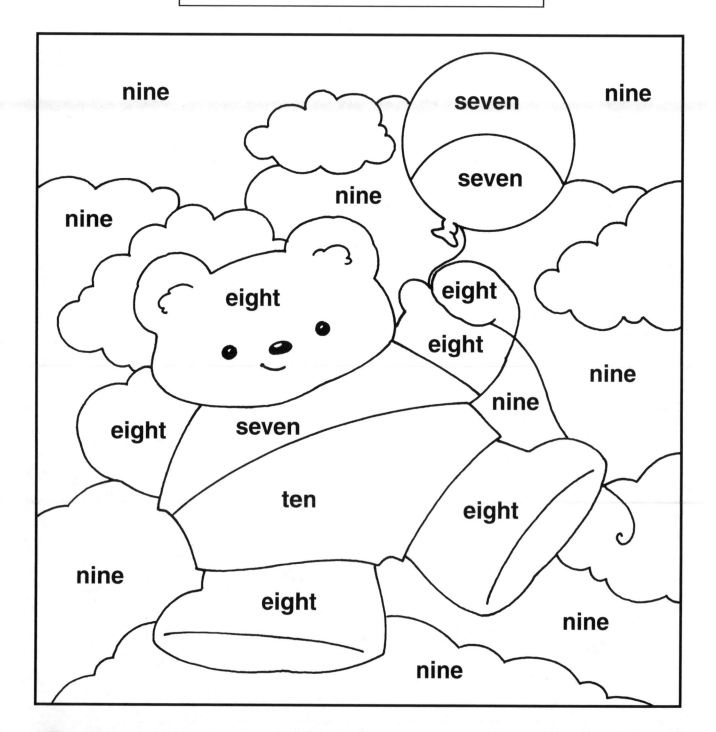

# Puzzle 12

## Farmer's Market

Read each number word. Color the puzzle.

| | | | |
|---|---|---|---|
| 11 = green | 12 = yellow | 13 = red | 14 = brown |

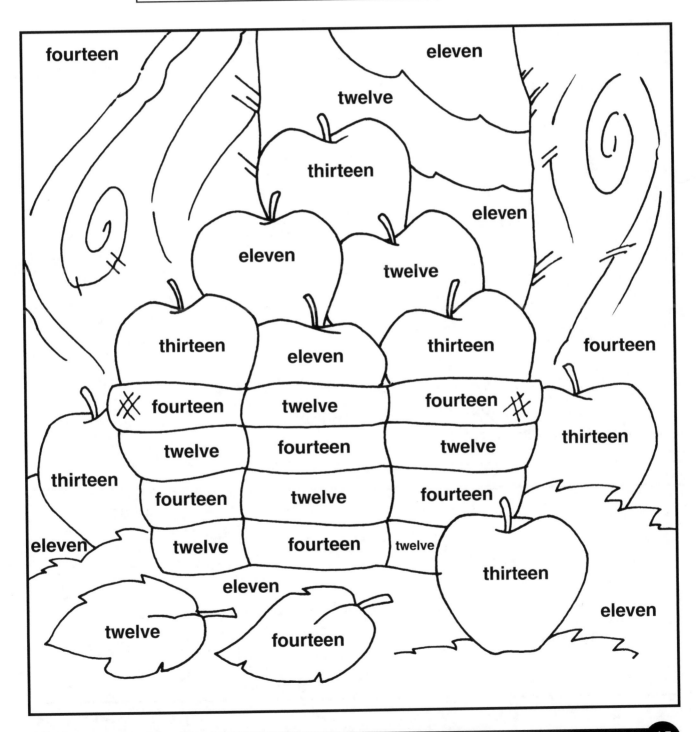

# Puzzle 13

## Double Scoops

Read each number word.  Color the puzzle.

| 14 = brown | 15 = pink | 16 = green | 17 = yellow |

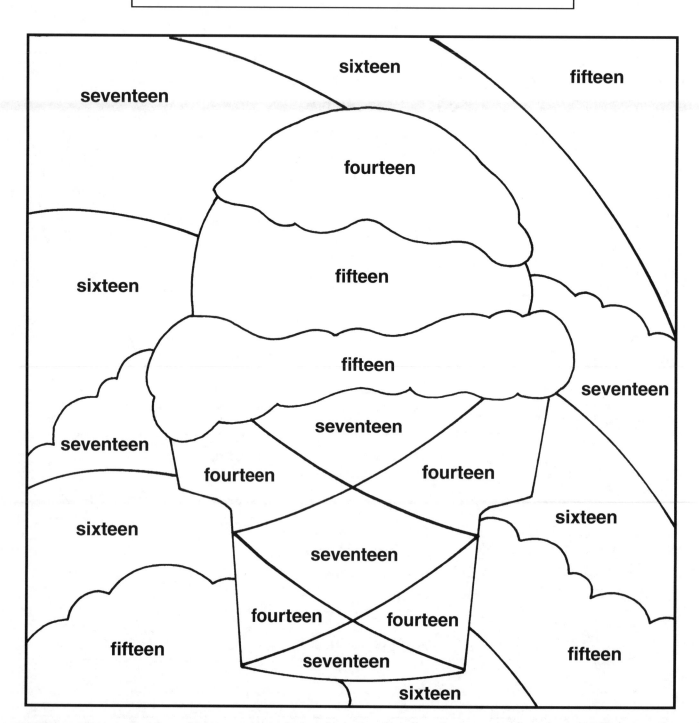

# Puzzle 14

## Robbie Robot

Read each number word.  Color the puzzle.

| 17 = gray    18 = red    19 = blue    20 = green |
| --- |

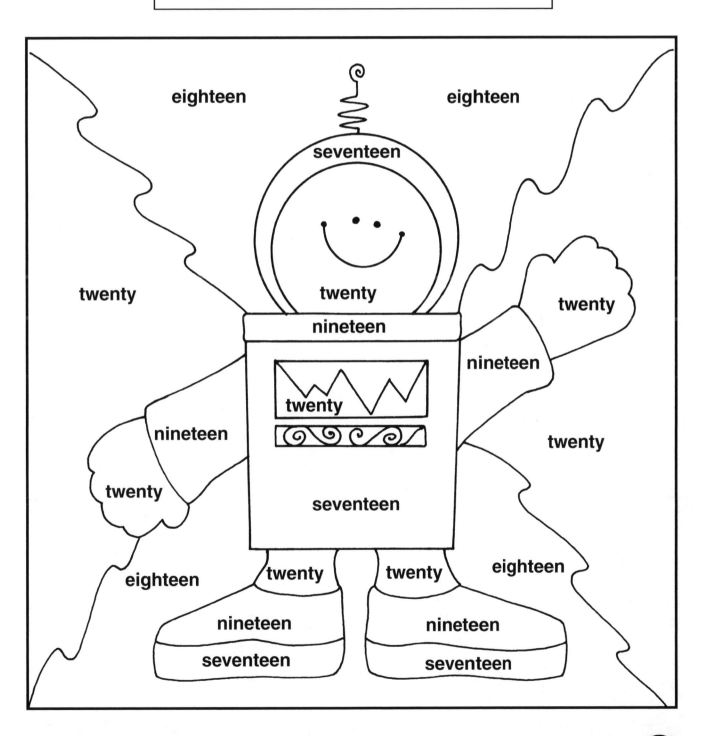

# Puzzle 15

## Busy as a Bee

Solve each addition problem.  Color the puzzle.

| 0 = yellow   1 = black   2 = blue   3 = green |
| --- |

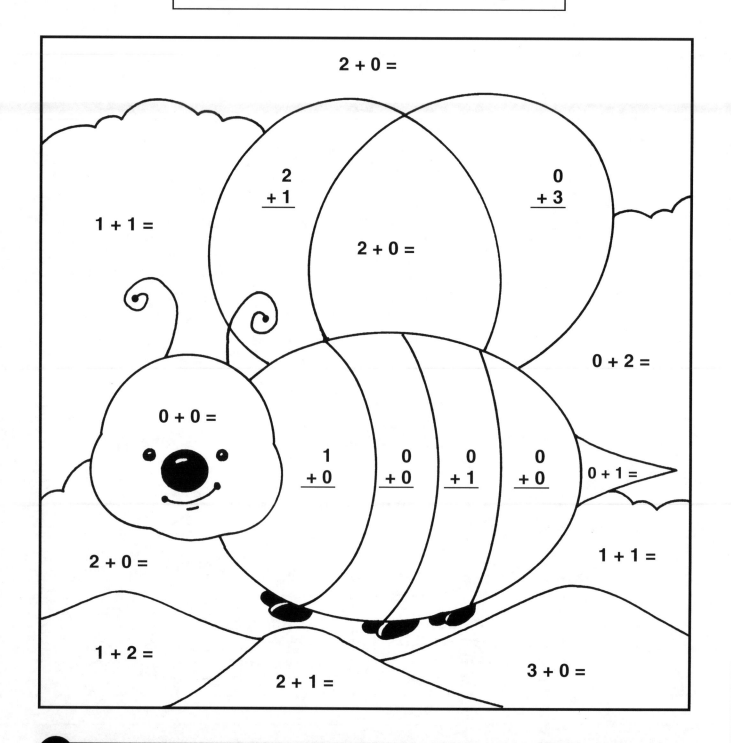

# Puzzle 16

## Home Sweet Home

Solve each addition problem. Color the puzzle.

| 4 = brown    5 = orange    6 = green |
| --- |

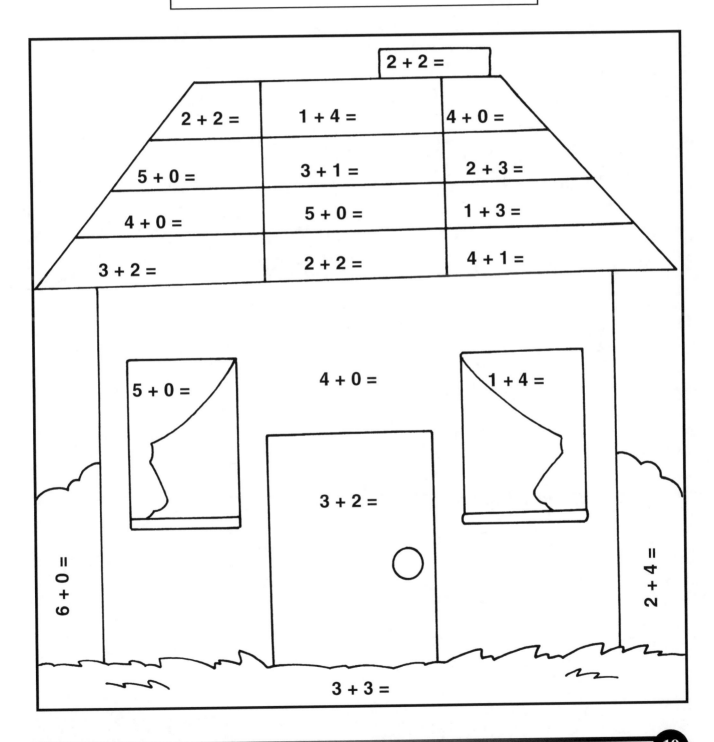

# Puzzle 17 ❧ ❧ ❧ ❧ ❧ ❧ ❧ ❧ ❧ ❧ ❧ ❧ ❧ ❧ ❧

## Fluttering By

Solve each addition problem.  Color the puzzle.

| 7 = orange   8 = yellow   9 = green   10 = blue |
|---|

2 + 8 =

10 + 0 =

2 + 5 =

5 + 5 =

4 + 3 =

3
+ 5

9 + 1 =

6 + 4 =

4 + 4 =

7 + 3 =

8 + 2 =

9 + 0 =

4 + 5 =

# Puzzle 18

## Buzzing Through the Numbers

Solve each addition problem. Color the puzzle.

| 11 = yellow 12 = brown 13 = purple 14 = blue |
| --- |

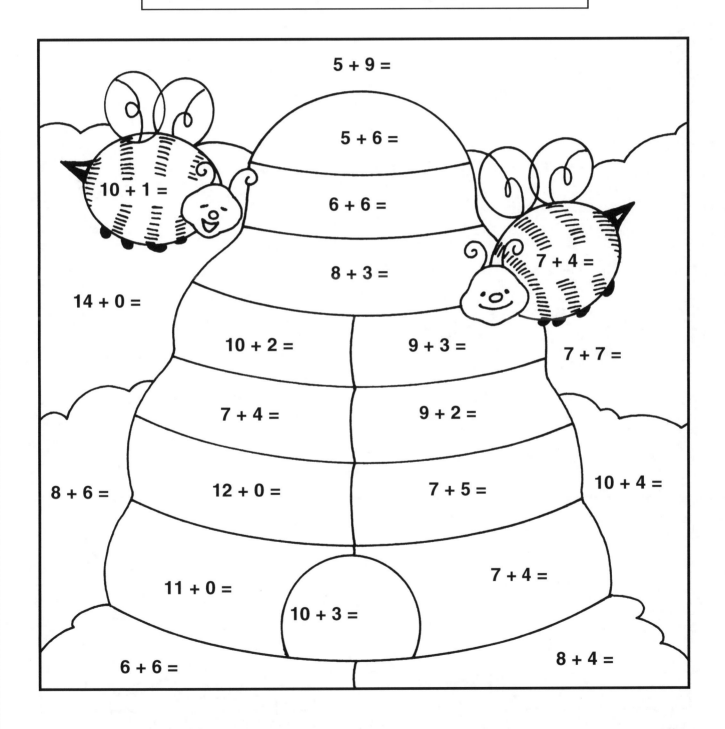

5 + 9 =

5 + 6 =

6 + 6 =

8 + 3 =

10 + 1 =

7 + 4 =

14 + 0 =

10 + 2 =    9 + 3 =

7 + 7 =

7 + 4 =    9 + 2 =

8 + 6 =    12 + 0 =    7 + 5 =    10 + 4 =

7 + 4 =

11 + 0 =

10 + 3 =

6 + 6 =    8 + 4 =

# Puzzle 19

## Over the Rainbow

Solve each subtraction problem.  Color the puzzle.

| 0 = red   1 = orange   2 = yellow   3 = blue |

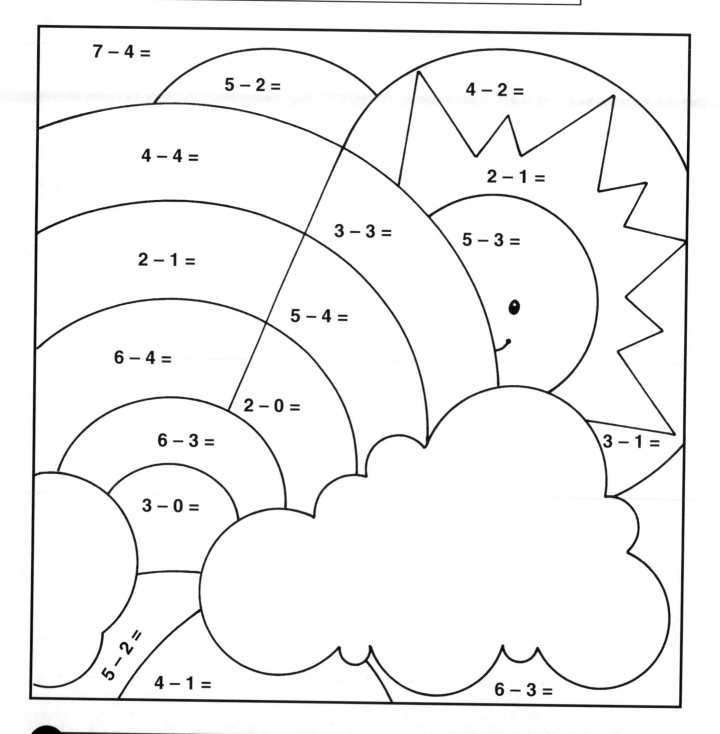

# Puzzle 20

## Blooming Buds

Solve each subtraction problem.  Color the puzzle.

| 4 = green   5 = orange   6 = purple   7 = yellow |

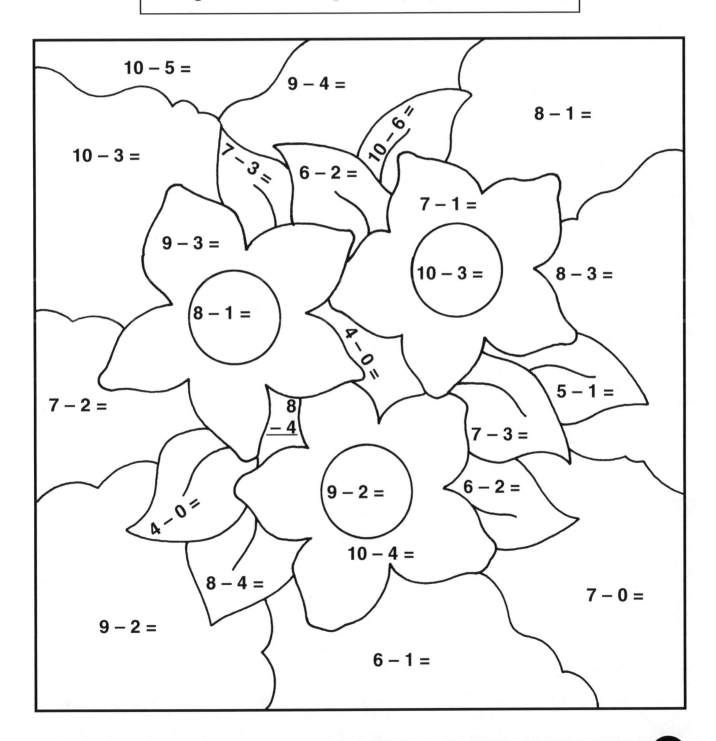

# Puzzle 21

## Camping Out

Solve each subtraction problem.  Color the puzzle.

| 8 = yellow | 9 = brown | 10 = red | 11 = green |
|---|---|---|---|

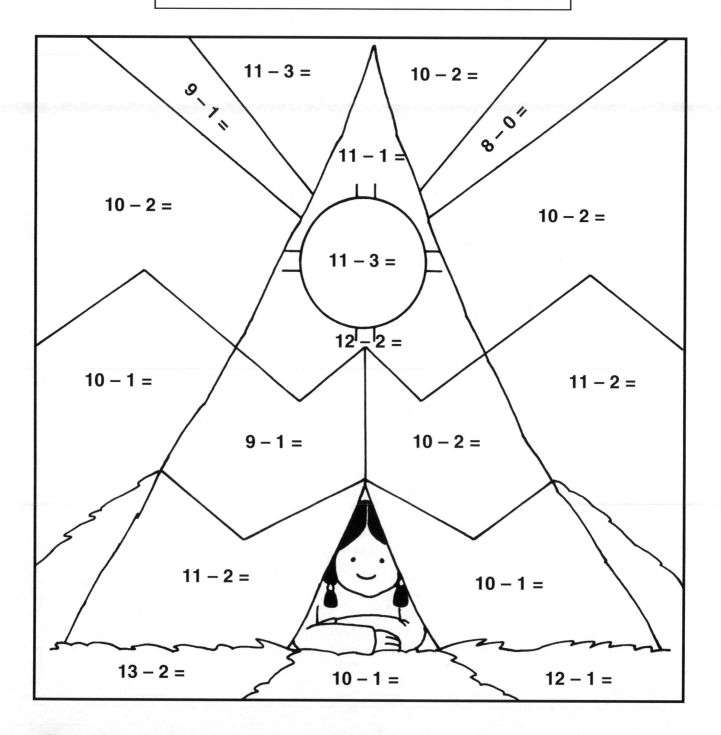

$11 - 3 =$

$10 - 2 =$

$9 - 1 =$

$8 - 0 =$

$11 - 1 =$

$10 - 2 =$

$10 - 2 =$

$11 - 3 =$

$12 - 2 =$

$10 - 1 =$

$11 - 2 =$

$9 - 1 =$

$10 - 2 =$

$11 - 2 =$

$10 - 1 =$

$13 - 2 =$

$10 - 1 =$

$12 - 1 =$

## Stripes for Dad

Color the puzzle.

urple   13 = green   14 = blue

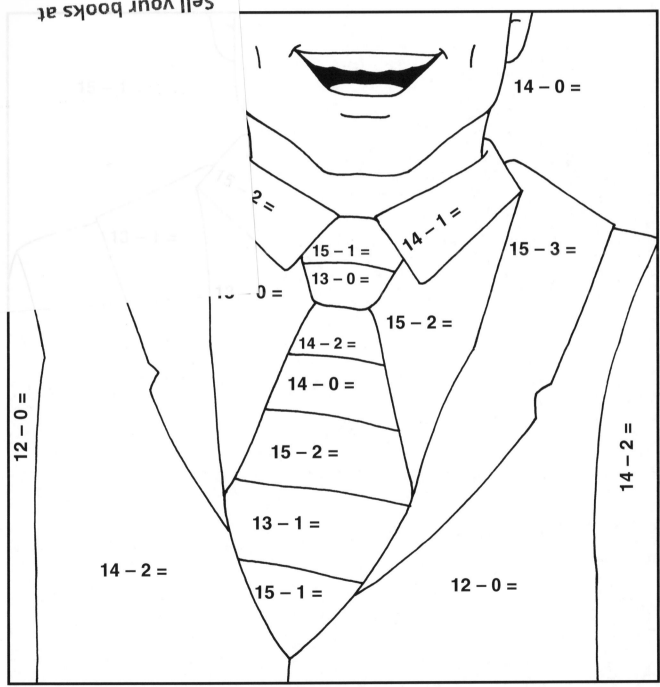

# Puzzle 23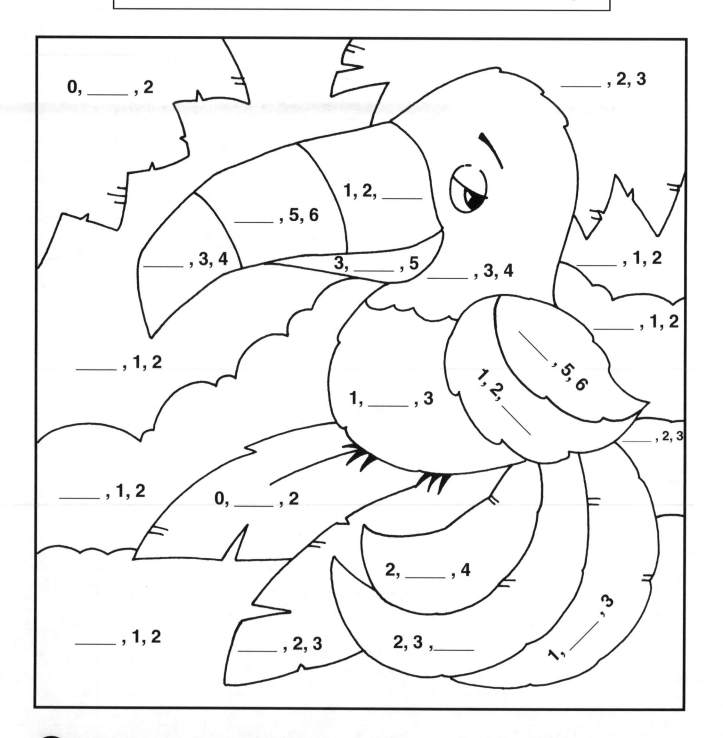

## Toucan Tom

Write the missing numbers.  Color the puzzle.

0 = blue   1 = green   2 = purple   3 = red   4 = orange

0, _____ , 2

_____ , 2, 3

1, 2, _____

_____ , 5, 6

_____ , 3, 4

3, _____ , 5

_____ , 3, 4

_____ , 1, 2

_____ , 1, 2

1, _____ , 3

1, 2, _____

_____ , 5, 6

_____ , 2, 3

_____ , 1, 2

0, _____ , 2

2, _____ , 4

_____ , 1, 2

_____ , 2, 3

2, 3 , _____

1, _____ , 3

# Puzzle 24

## Box Full of Colors

Write the missing numbers.  Color the puzzle.

| 5 = red   6 = orange   7 = yellow   8 = brown   9 = green |

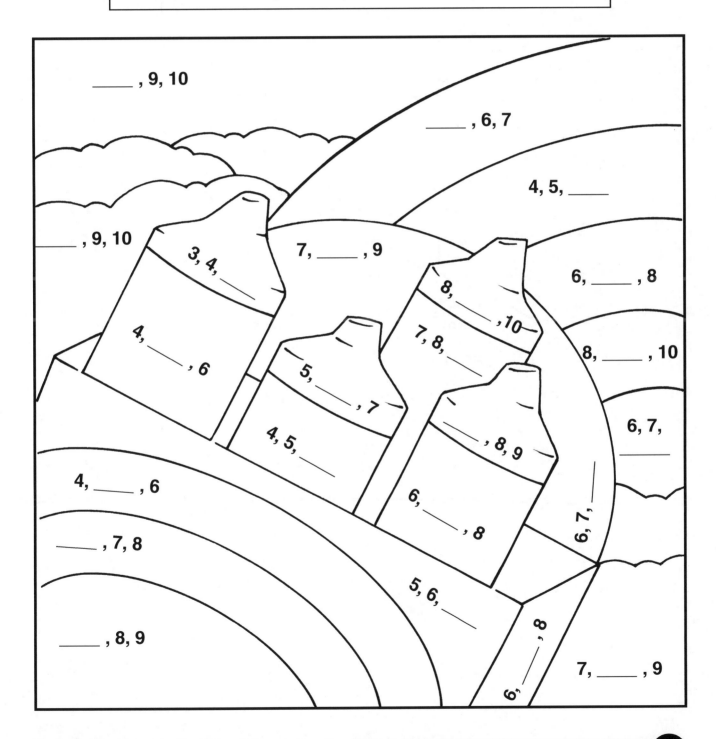

_____ , 9, 10

_____ , 6, 7

4, 5, _____

_____ , 9, 10

3, 4, _____

7, _____ , 9

8, _____ , 10

6, _____ , 8

7, 8, _____

4, _____ , 6

5, _____ , 7

8, _____ , 10

6, 7, _____

4, 5, _____

_____ , 8, 9

6, 7, _____

4, _____ , 6

6, _____ , 8

5, 6, _____

_____ , 7, 8

_____ , 8

_____ , 8, 9

6, _____

7, _____ , 9

# Puzzle 25 

## Take Note!

Write the missing numbers.  Color the puzzle.

| 10 = red | 11 = brown | 12 = yellow | 13 = pink | 14 = blue |
| --- | --- | --- | --- | --- |

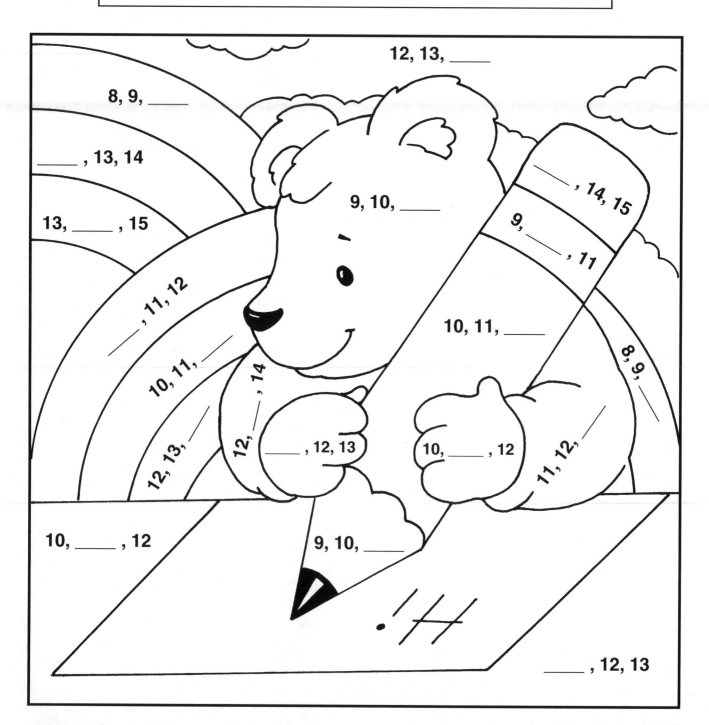

12, 13, _____

8, 9, _____

_____ , 13, 14

13, _____ , 15

_____ , 11, 12

10, 11, _____

12, 13, _____

_____ , 14

12, _____ , 13

10, _____ , 12

9, 10, _____

_____ , 14, 15

9, _____ , 11

10, 11, _____

8, 9, _____

10, _____ , 12

11, 12, _____

10, _____ , 12

9, 10, _____

_____ , 12, 13

# Puzzle 26

## Rat-A-Tat-Tat

Write the missing numbers.  Color the puzzle.

| 15 = orange | 16 = brown | 17 = purple | 18 = red | 19 = blue | 20 = yellow |

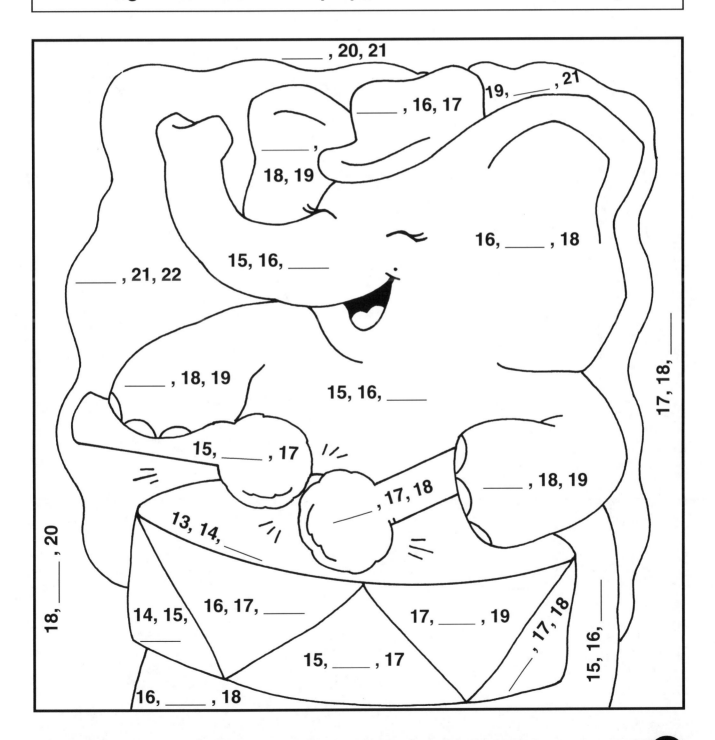

# Puzzle 27

## Pennies, Nickels, and Dimes

Determine the value of each coin. Color the puzzle.

1¢ = pink    5¢ = green    10¢ = blue

# Puzzle 28

## Money on the Flag

Determine the value of each coin.  Color the puzzle.

| 1¢ = black   5¢ = blue   10¢ = white   25¢ = red |
| --- |

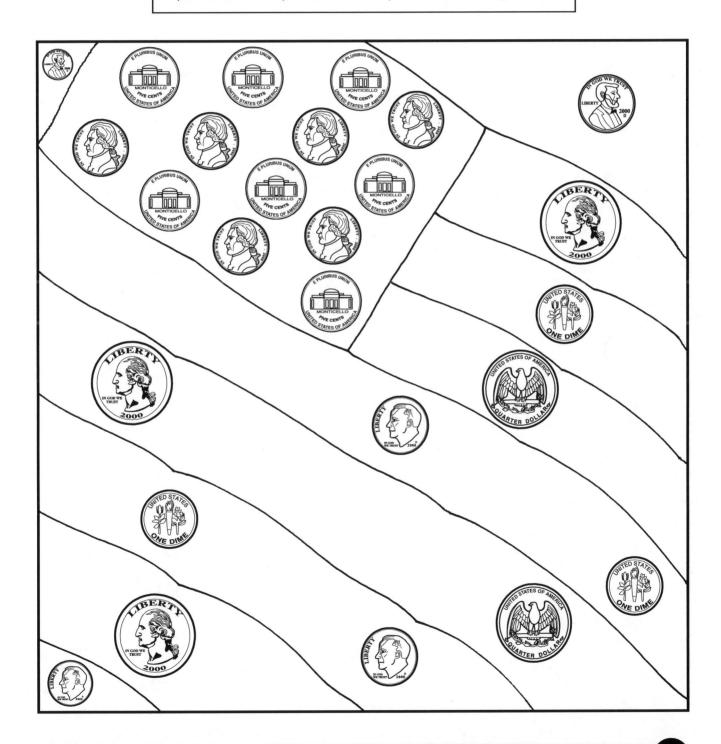

# Puzzle 29

## Follow the Arrow

Solve each problem. Color the puzzle.

0 = brown   1 = red   2 = green   3 = blue   4 = yellow

# Puzzle 30

## Blast Off!

Solve each problem. Color the puzzle.

| 5 = blue   6 = red   7 = gray   8 = purple |
|---|

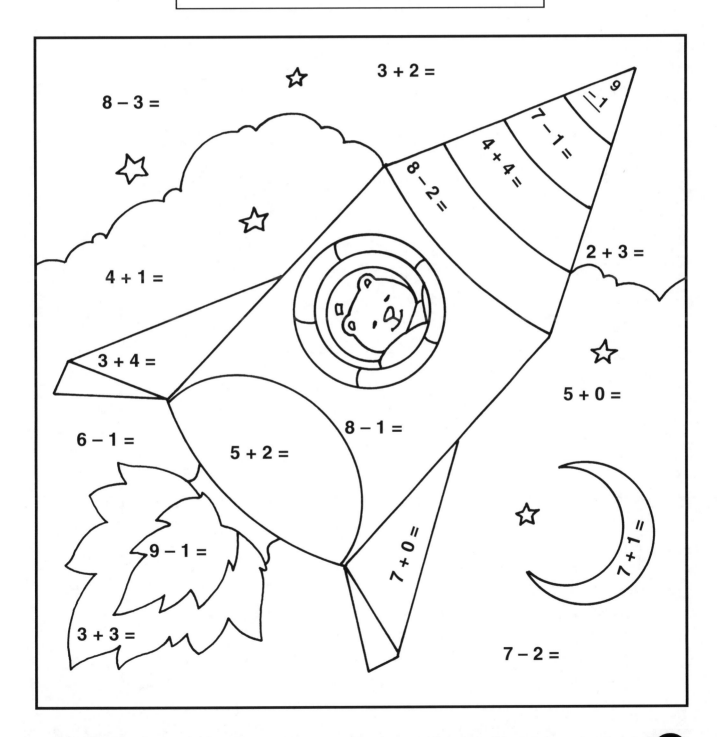

# Puzzle 31 🐚 🐚 🐚 🐚 🐚 🐚 🐚 🐚 🐚 🐚 🐚 🐚 🐚 🐚

## At the Barn

Solve each problem.  Color the puzzle.

| 9 = brown    10 = yellow    11 = red    12 = pink |

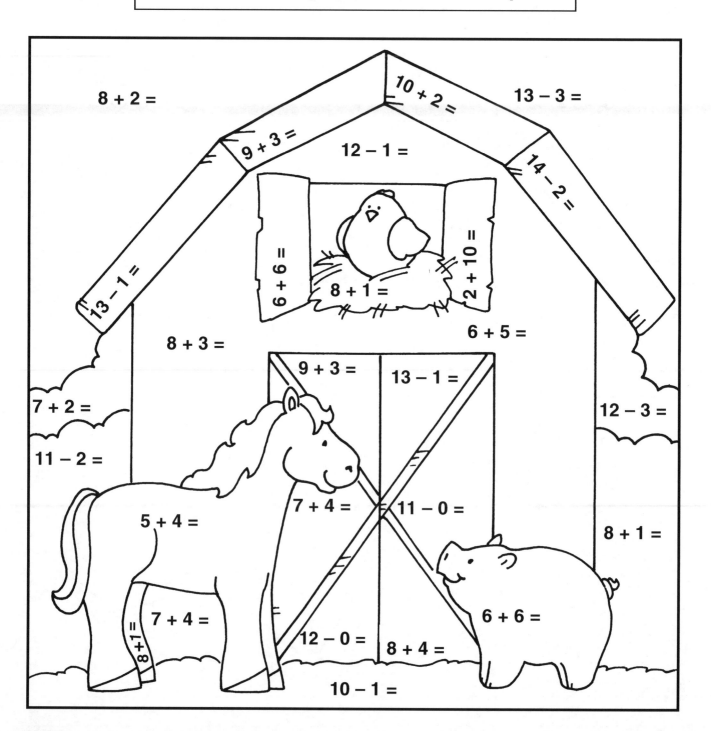

# Puzzle 32

## On the Road

Solve each problem.  Color the puzzle.

| 13 = green    14 = orange    15 = black    16 = blue |
|---|

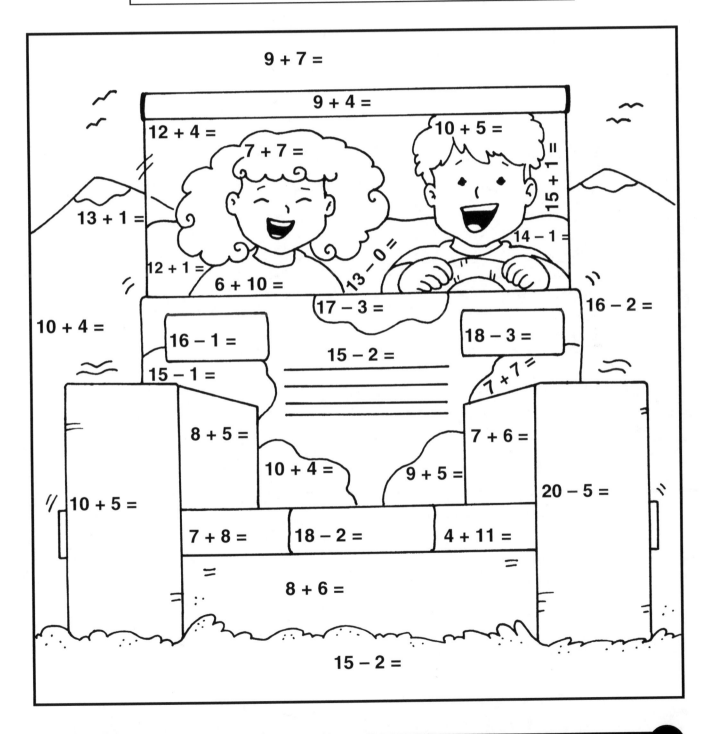

# Puzzle 33

## Odd and Even

Decide which numbers are odd and even.  Color the puzzle.

odd = red   even = blue

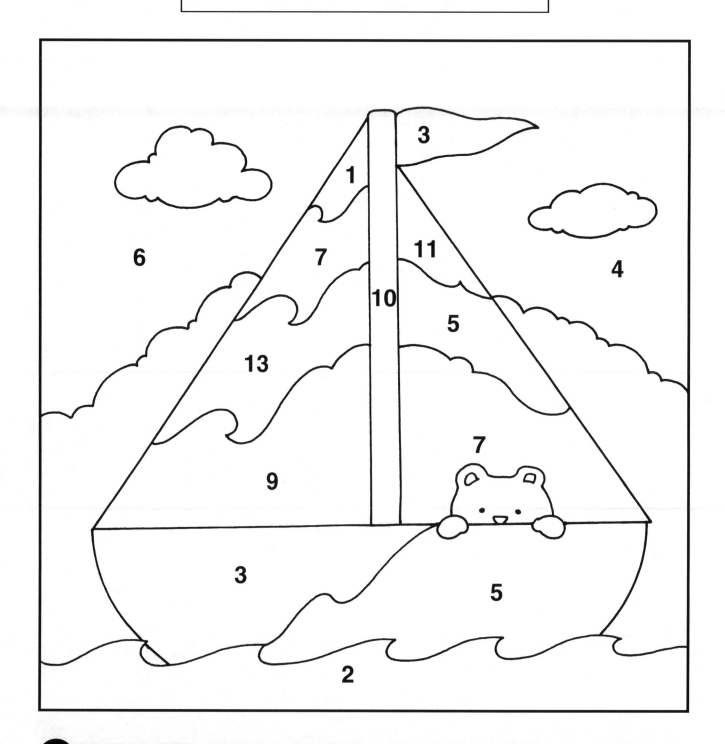

# Puzzle 34

## The Opposite Twins

Decide which numbers are odd and even. Color the puzzle.

odd = yellow    even = orange

# Puzzle 35

## By the 2's

Complete each number pattern.  Color the puzzle.

> 2 = yellow    4 = purple    6 = blue    8 = green    10 = red

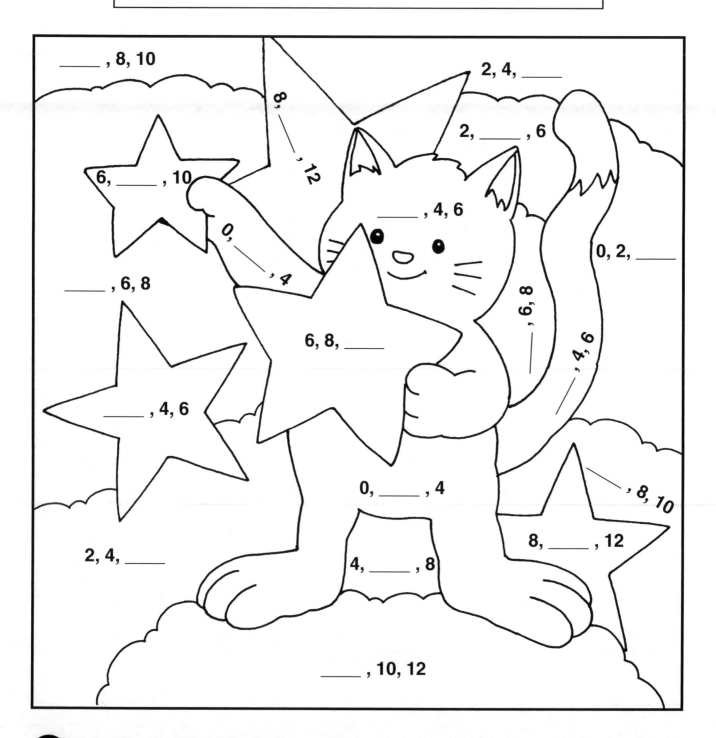

# Puzzle 36

## It's Heavy!

Complete each number pattern.  Color the puzzle.

| 5 = red    10 = blue    15 = green    20 = purple    25 = brown |

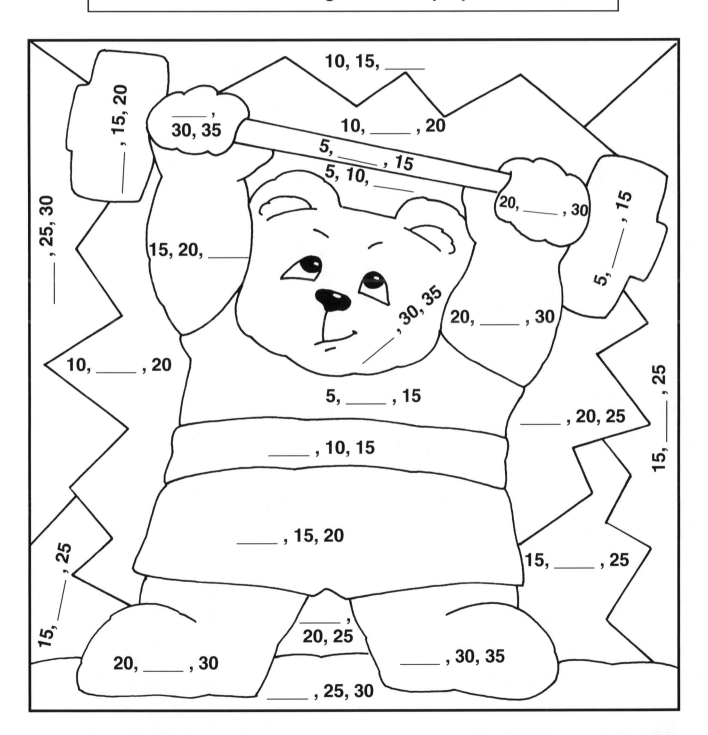

# Puzzle 37

## Give a Cheer!

Complete each number pattern. Color the puzzle.

| 10 = red  20 = brown  30 = green  40 = orange |

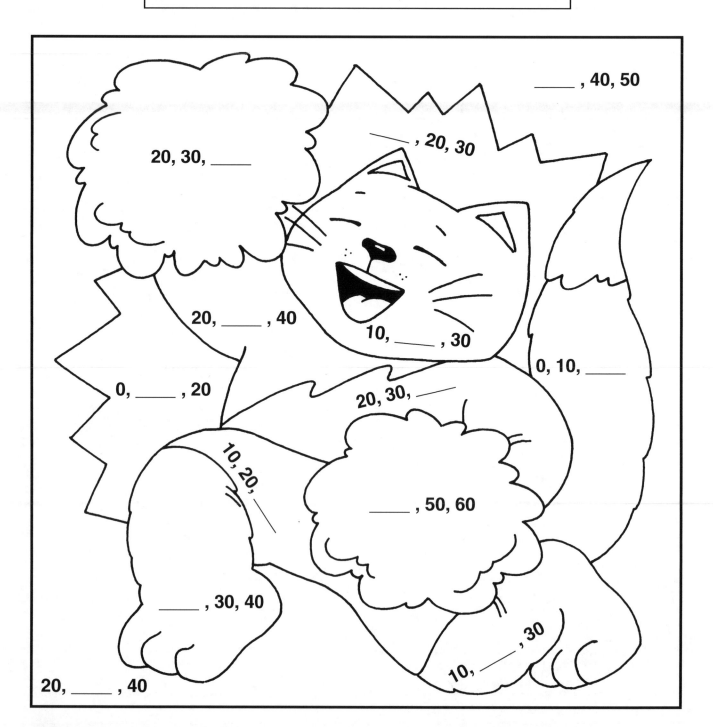

_____, 40, 50

_____, 20, 30

20, 30, _____

20, _____, 40

10, _____, 30

0, 10, _____

0, _____, 20

20, 30, _____

10, 20, _____

_____, 50, 60

_____, 30, 40

_____, 30

20, _____, 40

10, _____, 30

# Puzzle 38

## On the Island

Complete each number pattern. Decide how you are counting. Color the puzzle.

> **Counting by 1 = blue**   **Counting by 2 = green**
> **Counting by 5 = yellow**   **Counting by 10 = brown**

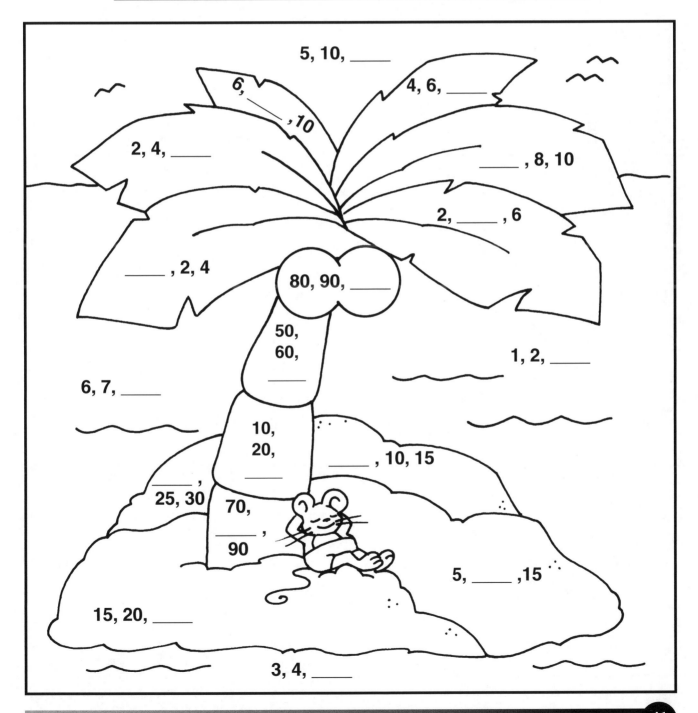

5, 10, _____

6, _____

_____, 10

4, 6, _____

2, 4, _____

_____, 8, 10

2, _____, 6

_____, 2, 4

80, 90, _____

50, 60, _____

1, 2, _____

6, 7, _____

10, 20, _____

_____, 10, 15

_____, 25, 30

70, _____, 90

5, _____, 15

15, 20, _____

3, 4, _____

# Answer Key

## Puzzle 1 Page 4

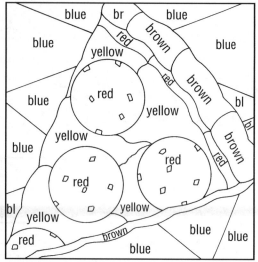

## Puzzle 2 Page 5

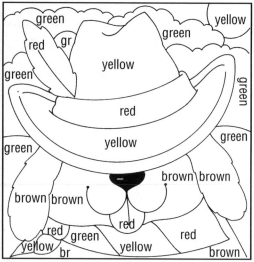

## Puzzle 3 Page 6

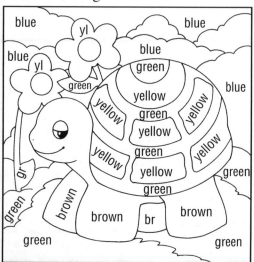

## Puzzle 4 Page 7

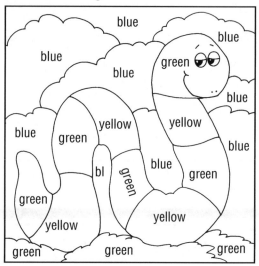

## Puzzle 5 Page 8

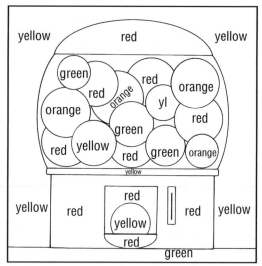

## Puzzle 6 Page 9

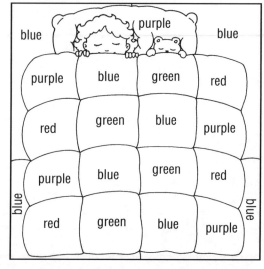

 #3906 Practice Makes Perfect: Math Picture Puzzles

# Answer Key

## Puzzle 7 Page 10

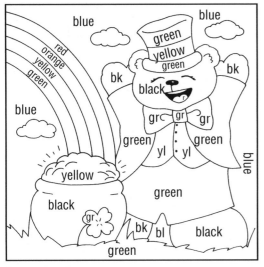

## Puzzle 8 Page 11

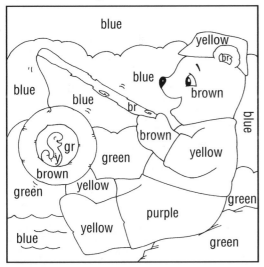

## Puzzle 9 Page 12

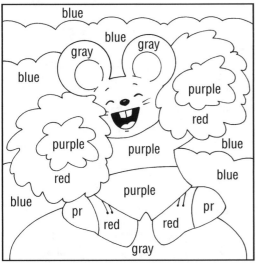

## Puzzle 10 Page 13

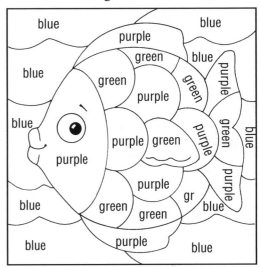

## Puzzle 11 Page 14

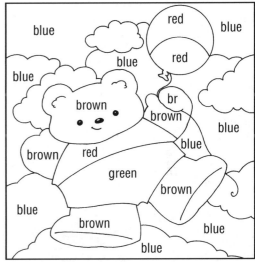

## Puzzle 12 Page 15

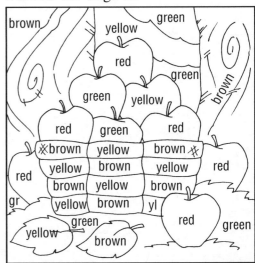

# Answer Key ♒ ◉ ♒ ◉ ♒ ◉ ♒ ◉ ♒ ◉ ♒ ◉ ♒ ◉.

**Puzzle 13**  Page 16

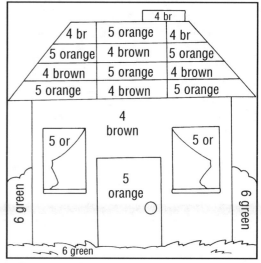

green  pink
yellow
brown
pink
green
pink
yellow
yellow yellow
brown   brown
green   green
yellow
brown  brown
pink   yellow   pink
green

**Puzzle 14**  Page 17

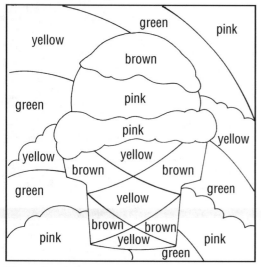

red          red
gray
green
green       green
blue
green  blue
blue
green
green  gray   green
green       red
red
blue   blue
gray   gray

**Puzzle 15**  Page 18

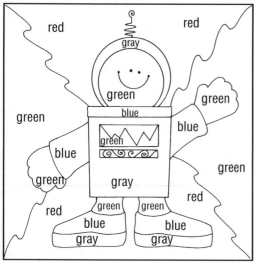

2 blue
3          3
2   green      green
blue     2
blue
2
blue
0        2
yellow   blue
1    0   1   0
black yellow black yellow  1 bk
2                        2
blue                     blue
3          3          3
green    green      green

**Puzzle 16**  Page 19

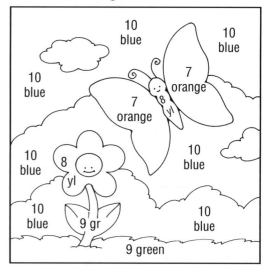

4 br
4 br    5 orange   4 br
5 orange  4 brown  5 orange
4 brown  5 orange  4 brown
5 orange  4 brown  5 orange
4
brown
5 or              5 or
5
orange
6 green                6 green
6 green

**Puzzle 17**  Page 20

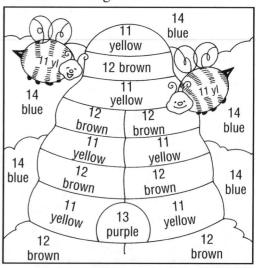

10            10
blue          blue
7
10         orange
blue
7         8
orange    yl
10
blue
10
blue      8
yl
10            10
blue          blue
9 gr
9 green

**Puzzle 18**  Page 21

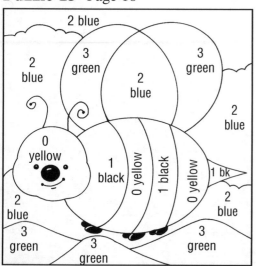

14
11    blue
yellow
11 yl   12 brown
11
14     yellow
blue               14
12      12      blue
brown   brown
14     11      11     14
blue  yellow  yellow  blue
12      12
brown   brown
11      11
yellow  13    yellow
purple
12                    12
brown                 brown

---

*#3906 Practice Makes Perfect: Math Picture Puzzles*          © *Teacher Created Resources, Inc.*

# Answer Key

**Puzzle 19** Page 22

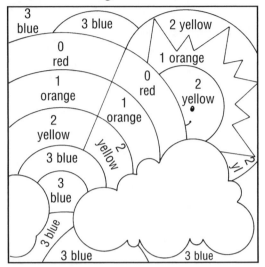

**Puzzle 20** Page 23

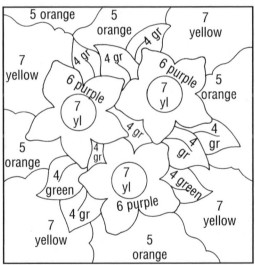

**Puzzle 21** Page 24

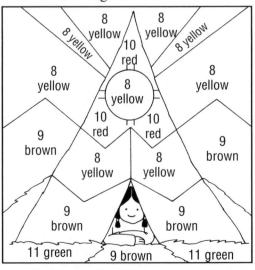

**Puzzle 22** Page 25

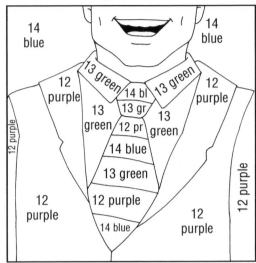

**Puzzle 23** Page 26

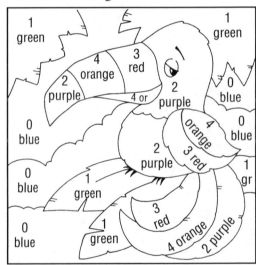

**Puzzle 24** Page 27

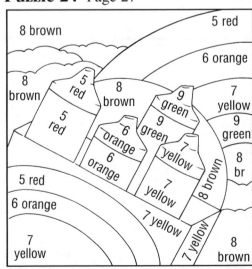

# Answer Key

## Puzzle 25  Page 28

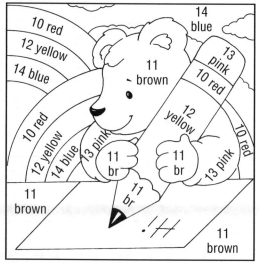

## Puzzle 26  Page 29

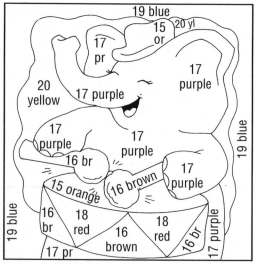

## Puzzle 27  Page 30

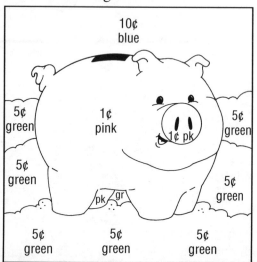

## Puzzle 28  Page 31

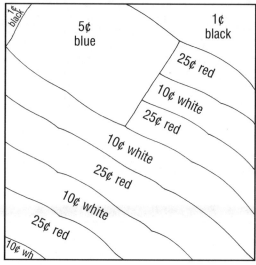

## Puzzle 29  Page 32

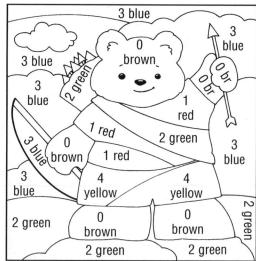

## Puzzle 30  Page 33

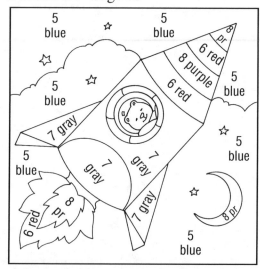

# Answer Key

## Puzzle 31  Page 34

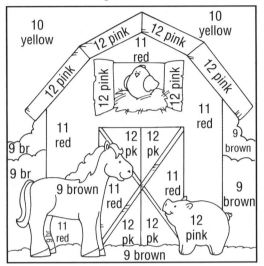

## Puzzle 32  Page 35

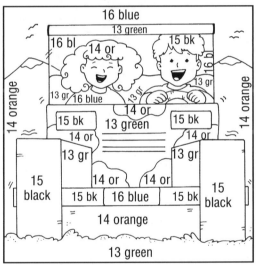

## Puzzle 33  Page 36

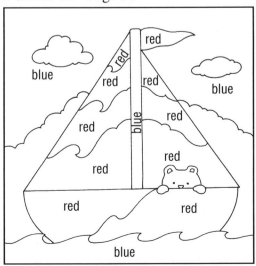

## Puzzle 34  Page 37

## Puzzle 35  Page 38

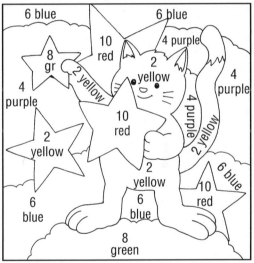

## Puzzle 36  Page 39

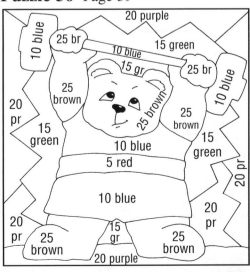

# Answer Key

**Puzzle 37** Page 40

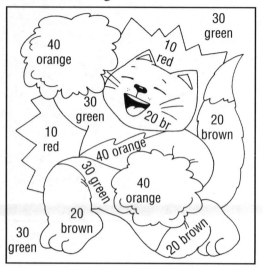

**Puzzle 38** Page 41

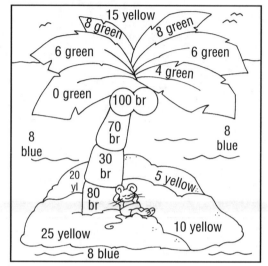